John Piper writes with a pastor's heart and a scholar's pen. This concise study makes for compelling reading, with its eloquent exploration of Wilberforce's Christian faith and the first principles that flowed from it. One cannot rightly understand Wilberforce's legacy as a reformer without understanding how his faith informed that legacy. Such a faith and such a legacy have much to say to us still. This is a book to savor and treasure.

—KEVIN BELMONTE, author of *William Wilberforce: A Hero for Humanity* and lead historical consultant for the motion picture *Amazing Grace: The William Wilberforce Story*

Amazing Grace in the Life of
William Wilberforce

John Piper

INTER-VARSITY PRESS
Norton Street, Nottingham NG7 3HR, England
Email: ivp@ivpbooks.com
Website: www.ivpbooks.com

First published 2007

British Library Cataloguing in Publication Data
A catalogue record for this book is available from the British Library.

ISBN 978-1-84474-185-4

Typeset in the USA
Printed in Great Britain

Inter-Varsity Press publishes Christian books that are true to the Bible and that communicate the gospel, develop discipleship and strengthen the church for its mission in the world.

Inter-Varsity Press is closely linked with the Universities and Colleges Christian Fellowship, a student movement connecting Christian Unions in universities and colleges throughout Great Britain, and a member movement of the International Fellowship of Evangelical Students. Website: ww.uccf.org.uk

Contents

The fatal habit of considering Christian morals as distinct from Christian doctrines insensibly gained strength. Thus the peculiar doctrines of Christianity went more and more out of sight, and as might naturally have been expected, the moral system itself also began to wither and decay, being robbed of that which should have supplied it with life and nutriment.

—WILLIAM WILBERFORCE

We can scarcely indeed look into any part of the sacred volume without meeting abundant proofs that it is the religion of the Affections which God particularly requires. . . . Joy . . . is enjoined on us as our bounden duty and commended to us as our acceptable worship. . . . A cold . . . unfeeling heart is represented as highly criminal.

—WILLIAM WILBERFORCE

If we would . . . rejoice in [Christ] as triumphantly as the first Christians did; we must learn, like them to repose our entire trust in him and to adopt the language of the apostle, "God forbid that I should glory, save in the cross of Jesus Christ. . . . Who of God is made unto us wisdom and righteousness and sanctification, and redemption."

—WILLIAM WILBERFORCE

His presence was as fatal to dullness as to immorality. His mirth was as irresistible as the first laughter of childhood.

—JAMES STEPHEN

Foreword

Jonathan Aitken

$\mathcal{E}$ven in the hands of a talented biographer, William Wilberforce is a difficult subject, for the story of his life can only be told with insights that transcend the writing of political history. The extraordinary tenacity he displayed over forty-six years of legislative warfare before the slave trade was abolished was an epic of Parliamentary perseverance. However, the real wellsprings of this momentous achievement are to be found not in votes counted, speeches delivered, or bills passed but in a far deeper level of spiritual and moral conviction.

John Piper has written a brilliant book because he so clearly understands that capturing the spirit and soul of William Wilberforce is crucial to portraying the man and his mission. The historical and political narrative of this account is impeccable, but the reader is also given a profoundly perceptive picture of how Wilberforce lived his life spiritually, from the inside. The artistry of this portrait results in a superlative biographical study that demonstrates the truth of the old adage: "A well-written life is as exceptional as a well lived one."

William Wilberforce did not always live his life well. In his youth he was a spoiled, selfish libertine who spent much of his time at the gaming tables playing poker. Having inherited a large fortune from his father, he could indulge his tastes for gambling as well as wining and dining in fashionable London clubs where he was also well known for his fine singing voice. Although he was more of a dilettante than anything else, he had some interest in politics. So when he was just twenty-one years old, he spent eight thousand pounds (equivalent to well over half-a-million dollars in today's money) on fighting and winning his home Parliamentary district of Hull in the 1780 general election. This was the start of a political career that was to change Britain and the world.

Having sat in the British House of Commons myself for nearly a quarter of a century, I know how easy it is for a young member of Parliament to fritter one's time away on empty debates and frustrating votes. There was nothing in Wilberforce's early days as a Parliamentarian to suggest that he was avoiding this familiar fate. As he himself described this period in his life, "The first years I was in Parliament I did nothing—nothing to any purpose. My own distinction was my darling object."

However, when Wilberforce was twenty-five years old, the whole direction of his life changed, not because of some new political appointment but because of a spiritual conversion that was so dramatic that he initially considered leaving Parliament to become a clergyman. Fortunately, a wise mentor, simply called "Old Newton" by Wilberforce, advised him against such a career change and urged him to remain in the House of Commons serving God through politics.

"Old Newton" was John Newton, the reformed slave ship captain who had become a minister in the Church of England, an author and writer of legendary hymns such as *Amazing Grace,* and a leader of the growing evangelical movement in eighteenth-century England. Newton had known William Wilberforce since Wilberforce was a thirteen-year-old school-boy. After the death of his parents, the orphaned Wilberforce was brought up by his aunt Hannah who was a close friend of Reverend and Mrs. Newton. Hannah was such an admirer of John Newton's sermons that she often went to hear them at his church in Olney, Buckinghamshire, sometimes staying in the vicarage accompanied by young William. So if the question is asked, who planted the first seed of Christian faith in the heart and mind of William Wilberforce, John Newton would be the most likely nomination. It seems inevitable that Newton's colorful life story and conversion would have made its mark on the teenaged Wilberforce during his visits to Olney and when Newton visited Hannah's hospitable home at Greenwich in South London.

As Newton's biographer, I fully concur with John Piper's assessment of the pivotal importance of the meeting between Wilberforce and Newton in December 1785. After a period of drifting away from the Christian faith in his locust years of idleness and gambling as a young man, Wilberforce was con-verted by his old schoolmaster, Isaac Milner, an evangelical friend of Newton's, during summer vacations on the French

Riviera in 1784 and 1785. But although he was on fire as a new convert, Wilberforce was disoriented. The culture of Parliament and the Church of England were hostile to evangelicals. Most of the high society to which he belonged sneered at the enthusiasm (a pejorative word in eighteenth-century English religion) with which evangelicals proclaimed the truth of the gospel. Yet this very truth and enthusiasm, which had brought Wilberforce into a relationship with Jesus Christ, was so powerful that he wanted to become an evangelical minister himself.

No wonder Wilberforce felt confused. He decided to pay a secret visit—secret because respectable members of Parliament should not be seen with despised evangelicals—to his aunt's old friend John Newton, who had recently been appointed Rector of St. Mary Woolnoth in the city of London. He was one of only two evangelical clergymen in the established church allowed charge of a London parish north of the River Thames.

Wilberforce's letter of December 2, 1785, to Newton requesting a meeting reads almost as if it comes from a spy making an undercover assignation with his controller.

> I wish to have some serious conversation with you. . . . I am sure you will hold yourself bound to let no-one living know of this application or of my visit till I release you from the obligation. . . . PS: Remember that I must be secret and that the gallery of the House is now so universally attended that the face of a member of parliament is pretty well known.

Wilberforce kept the appointment he had requested on

December 7, first taking the precaution of walking twice round the square in which Newton lived before knocking on the door of his home. Despite these cloak-and-dagger preliminaries, the meeting had transparent consequences in both the short and long term. According to Wilberforce, "When I came away I found myself in a calm tranquil state, more humbled and looking more devoutly up to God." According to Newton, he advised Wilberforce to remain in Parliament, later writing to tell him: "It is hoped and believed that the Lord has raised you up for the good of His church and for the good of the nation." John Piper's comment on this crucial conversation cannot be bettered:

> When one thinks what hung in the balance in that moment of counsel, one marvels at the magnitude of some small occasions in view of what Wilberforce would accomplish for the cause of abolition. (pp 30)

Abolishing the African slave trade became for Wilberforce "The grand object of my parliamentary existence. . . . If it please God to know me so far may I be the instrument of stopping such a course of wickedness and cruelty as never before disgraced a Christian country."

Wilberforce launched his campaign for abolition in 1787. He lived to see it finally succeed in 1833. For the first twenty years of his Parliamentary struggles he suffered nothing but defeats, insults, rejection from his friends, vilification from his enemies, and even threats to his life. In the history of British politics there has been no comparable display of moral courage over such a prolonged period by a single campaigner. Perhaps Winston Churchill's lonely opposition to the appeasement of Hitler's Germany in the 1930s comes close, but his wilderness years were shorter than those endured by Wilberforce and were thwarted by fewer defeats.

The bills to abolish the slave trade that Wilberforce presented to Parliament between 1787 and 1807 were voted down no less than eleven times. Moreover, the outside pressures on him to drop his campaign were formidable, for Wilberforce was challenging the vested interests of an immense trade that was vital to the British economy because of the wealth and jobs it created for ports, ship owners, shipbuilders, seafarers, traders, exporters of manufactured goods to Africa, and importers of cargoes from the West Indies. There was also fierce international opposition to Wilberforce from plantation owners and slave traders in America and from the West Indian colonial assemblies, which threatened to declare independence from England and to federate with the United States. The political hostility to Wilberforce sometimes erupted into personal hatred. He had to endure insults, slurs, slanders, and even threats on his life from one enraged slave ship captain.

Edmund Burke, Wilberforce's Parliamentary contemporary, once said: "One man with conviction makes a majority." It was a remark tailor-made to suit Wilberforce, for by the courage of his convictions he gradually swung Parliamentary and public opinion around to support the abolitionist cause. As Piper emphasizes, Wilberforce was blessed by the support of many staunch Christians among his allies, notably the influential members of the Clapham Sect in South London. He was also assisted by expert eyewitnesses who could testify about the horrors of the slave trade. John Newton's memorable evidence to the Privy Council, as the Cabinet was called in those days, was one of the leading testimonies that helped to turn the tide of the abolitionist campaign towards success.

The great breakthrough came in February 1807 when, at the twelfth attempt, the Bill for Abolition was carried in the House of Commons by the unexpectedly huge majority of 267 votes. As a prominent member of Parliament praised him for "having preserved so many of his fellow creatures," Wilberforce sat amidst the loud "hurrahs" and "hear hears" of his colleagues with head bowed, tears streaming down his face. After twenty years of defeats, with this victory he had changed the course of history.

There was still more work to be done, for although the slave *trade* had now been made illegal, slavery itself remained lawful for another twenty-six years. But Wilberforce remained a determined campaigner, and three months before his death he lived to see slavery outlawed by the final piece of abolitionist legislation, which was passed in 1833.

John Piper writes in his assessment of Wilberforce's amazing perseverance: "What drew me to Wilberforce in the first place [was] his reputation as a man who simply would not give up when the cause was just" (pp. 43). Because of this fundamental attraction of the author to his subject, perhaps the most fascinating chapters of this biographical study are those which focus on Wilberforce's motivation and dedication for his cause. Unlike most previous Wilberforce biographers, John Piper begins the account of his subject's life with an illuminating answer to the question: what made him tick? According to Piper, it was "a profound biblical allegiance" (pp. 20). Piper adds, "He was not a political pragmatist. He was a radically God-centered Christian who was a politician" (pp. 24). This explanation of Wilberforce's character and convictions is borne out by a careful analysis of the book he wrote at the age of thirty-seven, *A Practical View of Christianity*. It becomes clear from this work that the primary driving force behind Wilberforce's legislative perseverance was not, like most politicians before and since, to pass laws that would bring benefits to society; it was to pass laws to eradicate the activities of society that were offensive to God.

Once this great passion of Wilberforce's life is understood, everything about his campaign to abolish slavery falls into place, especially his extraordinary endurance in the face of disappointments, defeats, illness, and family problems. But perhaps the most enthralling chapter in this book is the penultimate one titled "The Deeper Root of Childlike Joy." For what Piper captures here is the infectious effervescent joy in Christ that radiated from Wilberforce, touching the hearts and lifting the spirits of almost everyone around him from his own young children to the establishment grandees of church and state. Inevitably Wilberforce was human enough to have his occasional down periods. Yet he was such a fighter for joy that he never ceased to win his battles and make his sacrifices as he reached the highest realms of all happiness—spiritual contentment in Christ.

John Piper's succinct and superbly perceptive study of William Wilberforce deserves to become an acclaimed bestseller, for it not only tells the story of a great man's life—it also tells us how to understand the ultimate source of his greatness and happiness. Moreover, that understanding goes far deeper than the abolitionist achievements for which Wilberforce is honored, astounding though they were. William Wilberforce's secret, as revealed in this book, was that he made the journey from self-centeredness, achievement-centeredness, and political-centeredness to God-centeredness. And he made it with Christlike joy.

Introduction:
Enduring for the Cause

Against great obstacles William Wilberforce, an evangelical member of Parliament, fought for the abolition of the African slave trade and against slavery itself until they were both illegal in the British empire. The battle consumed almost forty-six years of his life (from 1787 to 1833). The defeats and setbacks along the way would have caused the ordinary politician to embrace a more popular cause. Though he never lost a parliamentary election from age twenty-one to sixty-five, the cause of abolishing the slave trade was defeated eleven times before its passage in 1807. And the battle for abolishing slavery itself did not gain the decisive victory until three days before he died in 1833. What were the roots of this man's endurance in the cause of public righteousness?

What Made Him Tick?

To understand and appreciate the life and labor of William Wilberforce, one of the wisest things to do is to read his book

A Practical View of Christianity first and then read biographies. The book was published in 1797 when Wilberforce was thirty-seven years old and had been a member of the British Parliament already for sixteen years. It proved incredibly popular for the time, going through five printings in six months and being translated into five foreign languages. The book makes crystal-clear what drives Wilberforce as a person and a politician. Hearing it from his own mouth, as it were, will make the reading of all the biographies more fruitful. They don't always put a premium on what he does. So it can easily be missed, if we don't read Wilberforce first.

What made Wilberforce tick was a profound biblical allegiance to what he called the "peculiar doctrines" of Christianity. These, he said, give rise in turn to true "affections" for spiritual things, which then break the power of pride and greed and fear and lead to transformed morals, which lead to the political welfare of the nation. No true Christian can endure in battling unrighteousness unless his heart is aflame with new spiritual affections, or passions. "Mere knowledge is confessedly too weak. The affections alone remain to supply the deficiency."[1] This is the key to public and political morality. "If . . . a principle of true Religion [the Spirit-given new affections] should . . . gain ground, there is no estimating the effects on public morals, and the consequent influence on our political welfare."[2]

---

[1] William Wilberforce, *A Practical View of Christianity*, ed. Kevin Charles Belmonte (Peabody, Mass.: Hendrickson Publishers, 1996), 51.
[2] Ibid., 211.

The Great Doer

But he was no ordinary pragmatist or political utilitarian, even though he was one of the most practical men of his day. Yes, he was a great doer. One of his biographers said, "He lacked time for half the good works in his mind."[3] James Stephen, who knew him well, remarked, "Factories did not spring up more rapidly in Leeds and Manchester than schemes of benevolence beneath his roof."[4] "No man," Wilberforce wrote, "has a right to be idle." "Where is it," he asked, "that in such a world as this, health, and leisure, and affluence may not find some ignorance to instruct, some wrong to redress, some want to supply, some misery to alleviate?"[5] In other words, he lived to do good—or as Jesus said, to let his light shine before men that they might see his good deeds and give glory to his Father in heaven (Matt. 5:16).

> There is little doubt that Wilberforce changed the moral outlook of Great Britain. . . . The reformation of manners [morals] grew into Victorian virtues and Wilberforce touched the world when he made goodness fashionable. . . . Contrast the late eighteenth century . . . with its loose morals and corrupt public life, with the mid-nineteenth century. Whatever its faults, nineteenth-century British public life became famous for its emphasis on character, morals, and justice and the British business world famous for integrity.[6]

---

[3] John Pollock, *Wilberforce* (London: Constable and Company, 1977), 223.
[4] Ibid.
[5] Wilberforce, *A Practical View of Christianity*, 90.
[6] Pollock, "A Man Who Changed His Times," in *Character Counts: Leadership Qualities in Washington, Wilberforce, Lincoln, and Solzhenitsyn*, ed. Os Guinness (Grand Rapids, Mich.: Baker Book House, 1999), 87.

But he was practical with a difference. He believed with all his heart that new affections for God were the key to new morals and lasting political reformation. And these new affections and this reformation did not come from mere ethical systems. They came from what he called the "peculiar doctrines" of Christianity. For Wilberforce, practical deeds were born in "peculiar doctrines." By that term he simply meant the central distinguishing doctrines of human depravity, divine judgment, the substitutionary work of Christ on the cross, justification by faith alone, regeneration by the Holy Spirit, and the practical necessity of fruit in a life devoted to good deeds.[7]

The Fatal Habit of Nominal Christians

He wrote his book to show that the "bulk"[8] of Christians in England were merely nominal because they had abandoned these doctrines in favor of a system of ethics and had thus lost the power of ethical life and the political welfare. He wrote:

> The fatal habit of considering Christian morals as distinct from Christian doctrines insensibly gained strength. Thus the peculiar doctrines of Christianity went more and more out of sight, and as might naturally have been expected, the moral system itself also began to wither and decay, being robbed of that which should have supplied it with life and nutriment.[9]

---

[7] "The grand radical defect in the practical system of these nominal Christians, is their forgetfulness of all the peculiar doctrines of the Religion which they profess—the corruption of human nature—the atonement of the Savior—the sanctifying influence of the Holy Spirit." Ibid., 162-63.

[8] His favorite word for the majority of nominal Christians in Britain in his day.

[9] Wilberforce, *A Practical View of Christianity*, 198.

He pled with nominal Christians of England not to turn "their eyes from the grand peculiarities of Christianity, [but] to keep these ever in view, as the pregnant principles whence all the rest must derive their origin, and receive their best support."[10]

Knowing that Wilberforce was a politician for most of his adult life, who never lost an election from the time he was twenty-one years old, we might be tempted to think that his motives were purely pragmatic—as if he should say, "If Christianity works to produce the political welfare, then use it." But that is not the spirit of his mind or his life. In fact, he believed that such pragmatism would ruin the very thing it sought, the reformation of culture.

The Decisive Direction of Sin: Vertical

Take the example of how people define sin. When considering the nature of sin, Wilberforce said, the vast bulk of Christians in England estimated the guilt of an action "not by the proportion in which, according to scripture, [actions] are offensive to God, but by that in which they are injurious to society."[11] Now, on the face of it that sounds noble, loving, and practical. Sin hurts people, so don't sin.

Wouldn't that definition of sin be good for society? But Wilberforce says, "Their slight notions of the guilt and evil of sin [reveal] an utter [lack] of all suitable reverence for the Divine Majesty. This principle [reverence for the Divine Majesty] is justly termed in Scripture, 'The beginning of wis-

---

10 Ibid., 70.
11 Ibid., 147.

dom' [Ps. 111:10]."[12] And without this wisdom, there will be no deep and lasting good done for man, spiritually or politically. Therefore, the supremacy of God's glory in all things is what he calls "the grand governing maxim" in all of life.[13] The good of society may never be put ahead of this. That would dishonor God and, paradoxically, defeat the good of society. For the good of society, the good of society must not be the primary good.

What's Wrong with Dueling?

A practical example of how his mind worked is shown in his approach to the practice of dueling. Wilberforce hated this folly—the practice that demanded that a man of honor accept a challenge to a duel when another felt insulted. Wilberforce's close friend, the Prime Minister William Pitt, actually fought a duel with George Tierney in 1798, and Wilberforce was shocked that the Prime Minister would risk his life and the nation in this way.[14] Many opposed it on its human unreasonableness. But Wilberforce wrote:

> It seems hardly to have been noticed in what chiefly consists its *essential* guilt; that it is a deliberate preference of the favor of man, before the favor and approbation of God, in *articulo mortis* ["at the point of death"], in an instance, wherein our own life, and that of a fellow creature are at

---

[12] Ibid., 149.
[13] Ibid., 81.
[14] Pollock, *Wilberforce*, 162.

stake, and wherein we run the risk of rushing into the presence of our Maker in the very act of offending him.[15]

In other words, offending God is the essential consideration, not killing a man or imperiling a nation. That is what made Wilberforce tick. He was not a political pragmatist. He was a radically God-centered Christian who was a politician. And his true affections for God based on the "peculiar doctrines" of Christianity were the roots of his endurance in the cause of justice.

---

[15] Wilberforce, *A Practical View of Christianity*, 115-16.

Chapter One

His Early Life

*W*ilberforce was born August 24, 1759, in Hull, England. His father died just before Wilberforce turned nine years old. He was sent to live with his uncle and aunt, William and Hannah, where he came under evangelical influences. His mother was more high church and was concerned her son was "turning Methodist." So she took him out of the boarding school where they had sent him and put him in another.[1] He had admired George Whitefield, John Wesley, and John Newton as a child. But soon he left all the influence of the evangelicals behind. At his new school, he said later, "I did nothing at all." That lifestyle continued through his years in St. John's College at Cambridge. He was able to live off his parents' wealth and get by with little work. He lost any interest in biblical religion and loved circulating among the social elite.

He became friends with his contemporary William Pitt,

---

[1] Pollock, *Wilberforce*, 5.

who in just a few years, at the age of twenty-four in 1783, became the Prime Minister of England. On a lark, Wilberforce stood for the seat in the House of Commons for his hometown of Hull in 1780 when he was twenty-one. He spent £8,000 on the election. The money and his incredible gift for speaking triumphed over both his opponents. Pitt said Wilberforce possessed "the greatest natural eloquence of all the men I ever knew."[2]

Thus began a forty-five year investment in the politics of England. He began it as a late-night, party-loving, upper-class unbeliever. He was single and would stay that way happily until he was thirty-seven years old. Then he met Barbara on April 15, 1797. He fell immediately in love. Within eight days he proposed to her, and on May 30 they were married, about six weeks after they met—and stayed married until William died thirty-six years later. In the first eight years of their marriage they had four sons and two daughters. We will come back to William as a family man, because it sheds light on his character and how he endured the political battles of the day.

"The Great Change": The Story of His Conversion

I have skipped over the most important thing—his conversion to a deep, Christian, evangelical faith. It is a great story of the providence of God pursuing a person through seemingly casual choices. On the long holidays when Parliament was not in session, Wilberforce would sometimes travel with friends or

---

[2] Pollock, "A Man Who Changed His Times," 78.

family. In the winter of 1784 when he was twenty-five, on an impulse he invited Isaac Milner, his former schoolmaster and friend from grammar school, who was now a tutor in Queens College, Cambridge, to go with him and his mother and sister to the French Riviera. To his amazement Milner turned out to be a convinced Christian without any of the stereotypes that Wilberforce had built up against evangelicals. They talked for hours about the Christian faith.

In another seemingly accidental turn, Wilberforce saw lying in the house where they were staying a copy of Philip Doddridge's *The Rise and Progress of Religion in the Soul* (1745). He asked Milner about it, and Milner said that it was "one of the best books ever written" and suggested they take it along and read it on the way home.[3] Wilberforce later ascribes to this book a huge influence on his conversion. When he arrived home in February 1785 he "had reached intellectual assent to the biblical view of man, God and Christ." But he would not yet have claimed what he later described as true Christianity. It was all intellectual. He pushed it to the back of his mind and went on with political and social life.

That summer Wilberforce traveled again with Milner, and they discussed the Greek New Testament for hours. Slowly his "intellectual assent became profound conviction."[4] One of the first manifestations of what he called "the great change"—the conversion—was the contempt he felt for his wealth and the

---

[3] Ibid., 34.
[4] Ibid., 37.

luxury he lived in, especially on these trips between Parliamentary sessions. Seeds were sown almost immediately at the beginning of his Christian life, it seems, of the later passion to help the poor and to turn all his inherited wealth and his naturally high station into a means of blessing the oppressed.

"Highly Dangerous Possessions"

Simplicity and generosity were the mark of his life. Much later, after he was married, he wrote, "By careful management, I should be able to give at least one-quarter of my income to the poor."[5] His sons reported that before he married he was giving away well over a fourth of his income, one year actually giving away £3,000 more than he made. He wrote that riches were, "considering them as in themselves, acceptable, but, from the infirmity of [our] nature, as highly dangerous possessions; and [we are to value] them chiefly not as instruments of luxury or splendor, but as affording the means of honoring [our] heavenly Benefactor, and lessening the miseries of mankind."[6] This was the way his mind worked: Everything in politics was for the alleviation of misery and the spread of happiness.

The Regret That Leads to Life

By October he was bemoaning the "shapeless idleness" of his past. He was thinking particularly of his time at Cambridge—

---

[5] Betty Steele Everett, *Freedom Fighter: The Story of William Wilberforce* (Fort Washington, PA: Christian Literature Crusade, 1994), 68.
[6] Wilberforce, *A Practical View of Christianity*, 113.

"the most valuable years of life wasted, and opportunities lost, which can never be recovered."[7] He had squandered his early years in Parliament as well: "The first years I was in Parliament I did nothing—nothing that is to any purpose. My own distinction was my darling object."[8] He was so ashamed of his prior life that he wrote with apparent overstatement, "I was filled with sorrow. I am sure that no human creature could suffer more than I did for some months. It seems indeed it quite affected my reason."[9] He was tormented about what his new Christianity meant for his public life. William Pitt tried to talk him out of becoming an evangelical and argued that this change would "render your talents useless both to yourself and mankind."[10]

Ten Thousand Doubts and Good Counsel

To resolve the anguish he felt over what to do with his life as a Christian, he resolved to risk seeing John Newton on December 7, 1785—a risk because Newton was an evangelical and not admired or esteemed by Wilberforce's colleagues in Parliament. He wrote to Newton on December 2:

> I wish to have some serious conversation with you. . . .
> I have had ten thousand doubts within myself, whether or
> not I should discover myself to you; but every argument
> against it has its foundation in pride. I am sure you will hold

---

[7] Robert Isaac Wilberforce and Samuel Wilberforce, *The Life of William Wilberforce*, Vol. 1 (London: John Murray, 1838), p. 107.
[8] Pollock, "A Man Who Changed His Times," 80.
[9] Pollock, *Wilberforce*, 37.
[10] Ibid., 38.

yourself bound to let no one living know of this application, or of my visit, till I release you from the obligation. . . . PS: Remember that I must be secret, and that the gallery of the House is now so universally attended, that the face of a member of parliament is pretty well known.[11]

It was a historically significant visit. Not only did Newton give encouragement to Wilberforce's faith, but he also urged him not to cut himself off from public life. Wilberforce wrote about the visit:

After walking about the Square once or twice before I could persuade myself, I called upon old Newton—was much affected in conversing with him—something very pleasing and unaffected in him. He told me he always had hopes and confidence that God would sometime bring me to Him. . . . When I came away I found my mind in a calm, tranquil state, more humbled, and looking more devoutly up to God.[12]

Wilberforce was relieved that the sixty-year-old Newton urged him not to cut himself off from public life. Newton wrote to Wilberforce two years later: "It is hoped and believed that the Lord has raised you up for the good of His church and for the good of the nation."[13] When one thinks what hung in the balance in that moment of counsel, one marvels at the magnitude

---

[11] Robert Isaac Wilberforce and Samuel Wilberforce, *The Life of William Wilberforce*, abridged edition (London, 1843), 47.
[12] Ibid., 48.
[13] Ibid.

of some small occasions in view of what Wilberforce would accomplish for the cause of abolition.

The battle and uncertainties lasted on into the new year, but finally a more settled serenity came over him, and on Easter Day 1786, the politician for Yorkshire took to the fields to pray and give thanks, as he said in a letter to his sister Sally, "amidst the general chorus with which all nature seems on such a morning to be swelling the song of praise and thanksgiving."[14] It was, he said almost ten years later, as if "to have awakened . . . from a dream, to have recovered, as it were, the use of my reason after a delirium."[15]

With this change came a whole new regimen for the use of his months of recess from Parliament. Beginning not long after his conversion and lasting until he was married eleven years later, he would now spend his days studying "about nine or ten hours a day," typically "breakfasting alone, taking walks alone, dining with the host family and other guests but not joining them in the evening until he 'came down about three-quarters of an hour before bedtime for what supper I wanted.'"[16] "The Bible became his best-loved book and he learned stretches by heart."[17] He was setting out to recover a lot of ground lost to laziness in college.

---

[14] Ibid., 39.
[15] Robert Isaac Wilberforce and Samuel Wilberforce, *The Life of William Wilberforce*, Vol. 1, 107-8.
[16] Ibid., 43.
[17] Ibid., 44.

Chapter Two

"God Has Set Before Me Two Great Objects"

*N*ow we turn to what makes Wilberforce so relevant to the cause of racial justice in our day—namely, his lifelong devotion to the cause of abolishing the African slave trade, and then slavery itself. In 1787 Wilberforce wrote a letter in which he estimated that the annual revenue from the export of slaves from the western coast of Africa for all nations exceeded £100,000.[1] Seventeen years later in 1804 he estimated that for the Guiana importation alone, 12,000 to 15,000 human beings were enslaved every year the trade continued. One year after his conversion, God's apparent calling on his life had become clear to him. On October 28, 1787, he wrote in his diary, "God Almighty has placed before me two great Objects, the Suppression of the Slave Trade and the Reformation of Manners [morals]."[2]

---

[1] Ibid., 72.
[2] Ibid., 69.

Soon after Christmas, 1787, a few days before the parliamentary recess, Wilberforce gave notice in the House of Commons that early in the new session he would bring a motion for the abolition of the slave trade. It would be twenty years before he could carry the House of Commons and the House of Lords in putting abolition into law. But the more he studied the matter and the more he heard of the atrocities, the more resolved he became. In May 1789 he spoke to the House about how he came to his conviction: "I confess to you, so enormous, so dreadful, so irremediable did its wickedness appear that my own mind was completely made up for Abolition. . . . Let the consequences be what they would, I from this time determined that I would never rest until I had effected its abolition."[3]

> He embraced the guilt for himself when he said in that same year, "I mean not to accuse anyone but to take the shame upon myself, in common indeed with the whole Parliament of Great Britain, for having suffered this horrid trade to be carried on under their authority. We are all guilty—we ought all to plead guilty, and not to exculpate ourselves by throwing the blame on others."[4]

In 1793 he wrote to a supporter who thought he was growing soft and cautious in the cause: "If I thought the immediate Abolition of the Slave Trade would cause an insurrection in our islands, I should not for an instant remit my most stren-

---

[3] Ibid., 56.
[4] Ibid., 89.

uous endeavors. Be persuaded then, I shall still less ever make this grand cause the sport of the caprice, or sacrifice it to motives of political convenience or personal feeling."[5] Three years later, almost ten years after the battle was begun, he wrote:

> The grand object of my parliamentary existence [is the abolition of the slave trade]. . . . Before this great cause all others dwindle in my eyes, and I must say that the *certainty* that I am right *here*, adds greatly to the complacency with which I exert myself in asserting it. If it please God to honor me so far, may I be the instrument of stopping such a course of wickedness and cruelty as never before disgraced a Christian country.[6]

Triumph over All Opposition

Of course the opposition that raged for these twenty years was because of the financial benefits of slavery to the traders and to the British economy, because of what the plantations in the West Indies produced. They could not conceive of any way to produce without slave labor. This meant that Wilberforce's life was threatened more than once. When he criticized the credibility of a slave ship captain, Robert Norris, the man was enraged, and Wilberforce feared for his life. Short of physical harm, there was the painful loss of friends. Some would no longer fight with him, and they were estranged. Then there was the huge political pressure to back down because of the

---

[5] Ibid., 123.
[6] Ibid., 143.

international political ramifications. For example, if Britain really outlawed slavery, the West Indian colonial assemblies threatened to declare independence from Britain and to federate with the United States. These kinds of financial and political arguments held Parliament captive for decades.

But the night—or I should say early morning—of victory came in 1807. The moral vision and the political momentum for abolition had finally become irresistible. At one point "the House rose almost to a man and turned towards Wilberforce in a burst of Parliamentary cheers. Suddenly, above the roar of 'Hear, hear,' and quite out of order, three hurrahs echoed and echoed while he sat, head bowed, tears streaming down his face."[7] At 4:00 A.M., February 24, 1807, the House divided—Ayes, 283, Noes, 16, Majority for the Abolition 267. And on March 25, 1807, the royal assent was declared. One of Wilberforce's friends wrote, "[Wilberforce] attributes it to the immediate interposition of Providence."[8] In that early morning hour Wilberforce turned to his best friend and colleague, Henry Thornton, and said, "Well, Henry, what shall we abolish next?"[9]

The Battle Was Not Over

Of course the battle wasn't over. And Wilberforce fought on[10] until his death twenty-six years later in 1833. Not only was the *implementation* of the abolition law controversial and dif-

---

[7] Ibid., 211.
[8] Ibid., 212.
[9] Ibid.
[10] In 1823 Wilberforce wrote a 56-page booklet, "Appeal to the Religion, Justice and Humanity of the Inhabitants of the British Empire in Behalf of the Negro Slaves in the West Indies." Ibid., 285.

ficult, but all it did was abolish the slave *trade*, not slavery itself. That became the next major cause. In 1821 Wilberforce recruited Thomas Fowell Buxton to carry on the fight, and from the sidelines, aged and fragile, he cheered him on. Three months before his death in 1833 he was persuaded to propose a last petition against slavery. "I had never thought to appear in public again, but it shall never be said that William Wilberforce is silent while the slaves require his help."[11]

The decisive vote of victory for that one came on July 26, 1833, only three days before Wilberforce died. Slavery itself was outlawed in the British colonies. Minor work on the legislation took several more days. "It is a singular fact," Buxton said, "that on the very night on which we were successfully engaged in the House of Commons, in passing the clause of the Act of Emancipation—one of the most important clauses ever enacted . . . the spirit of our friend left the world. The day which was the termination of his labors was the termination of his life."[12]

William Cowper wrote a sonnet[13] to celebrate Wilberforce's labor for the slaves which begins with the lines,

---

[11] Pollock, "A Man Who Changed His Times," 90.

[12] Ibid., 91.

[13] *Thy country, Wilberforce, with just disdain*
Hears thee by cruel men and impious call'd
Fanatic, for thy zeal to loose the enthrall'd
From exile, public sale, and slavery's chain.
Friend of the poor, the wrong'd, the fetter-gall'd,
Fear not lest labor such as thine be vain.
Thou hast achieved a part: hast gained the ear
Of Britain's senate to thy glorious cause;
Hope smiles, joy springs; and though cold Caution pause,
And weave delay, the better hour is near
That shall remunerate thy toils severe,
By peace for Afric, fenced with British laws.
Enjoy what thou has won, esteem and love
From all the Just on earth, and all the Blest above.

Thy country, Wilberforce, with just disdain,
Hears thee by cruel men and impious call'd
Fanatic, for thy zeal to loose the enthrall'd
From exile, public sale, and slavery's chain.
Friend of the poor, the wrong'd, the fetter-gall'd,
Fear not lest labor such as thine be vain.

Wilberforce's friend and sometimes pastor, William Jay, wrote a tribute with this accurate prophecy: "His disinterested, self-denying, laborious, undeclining efforts in this cause of justice and humanity . . . will call down the blessings of millions; and ages yet to come will glory in his memory."[14]

---

[14] William Jay, *The Autobiography of William Jay*, ed. George Redford and John Angell James (Edinburgh: The Banner of Truth Trust, 1974, orig. 1854), 315.

Chapter Three

A Multitude of Christlike Causes

I must not give the impression that all Wilberforce cared about or worked for was the abolition of slavery. In fact, the diversity of the evangelistic and benevolent causes he labored to advance makes his devotion to abolition all the more wonderful. Most of us make the multiplicity of demands an excuse for not giving ourselves to any one great cause over the long haul. Not so with Wilberforce.[1] There was a steady stream of action to alleviate pain and bring the greater social (and eternal!) good. "At one stage he was active in sixty-nine different initiatives."[2]

His involvements ranged widely. He was involved with the British Foreign Bible Society, the Church Missionary Society, the Society for the Manufacturing Poor, and the Society for the Better Observance of Sunday. He worked for the alleviation

---

[1] See 21-22.
[2] Pollock, "A Man Who Changed His Times," 89.

of harsh child labor conditions (like the use of small boys by chimney sweeps to climb up chimneys), for agricultural reform that supplied affordable food to the poor, for prison reform and the restriction of capital punishment from cavalier use, and for the prevention of cruelty to animals.[3] On and on the list could go. In fact, it was the very diversity of the needs and crimes and injustices that confirmed his evangelical conviction that one must finally deal with the root of all these ills if one is to have a lasting and broad influence for good. That is why, as we have seen, he wrote his book *A Practical View of Christianity*.

The Personal Evangelism of a Politician

Alongside all his social engagements, he carried on a steady relational ministry, as we might call it, seeking to win his unbelieving colleagues to personal faith in Jesus Christ. Even though he said, "the grand business of [clergymen's] lives should be winning souls from the power of Satan unto God, and compared with it all other pursuits are mean and contemptible,"[4] he did not believe that this was the responsibility

---

[3] Of course, concern for animals is not the apex of the moral life. But it may be indicative of a character that supports far more significant mercies. As the Scripture says, "Whoever is righteous has regard for the life of his beast, but the mercy of the wicked is cruel" (Prov. 12:10). So the following personal recollection of Wilberforce's grandson is not insignificant. "Wilberforce was also a great lover of animals and a founder of the Royal Society for the Prevention of Cruelty to Animals, which led me to a lovely story. His last surviving grandson told me how his father as a small boy was walking with Wilberforce on a hill near Bath when they saw a poor carthorse being cruelly whipped by the carter as he struggled to pull a load of stone up the hill. The little liberator expostulated with the carter who began to swear at him and tell him to mind his own business, and so forth. Suddenly the carter stopped and said, 'Are you Mr. Wilberforce? . . . Then I will never beat my horse again!'" Pollock, "A Man Who Changed His Times," 90.
[4] Pollock, *Wilberforce*, 148.

only of the clergy. In a chance meeting with James Boswell, Samuel Johnson's biographer, he spent time into the night dealing with him about his soul, but seemed not to be able to get beyond some serious feelings.[5] He grieved for his longtime unbelieving parliamentary friend Charles Fox and longed "that I might be the instrument of bringing him to the knowledge of Christ!"[6]

He anonymously visited in prison a famous infidel named Richard Carlile who was imprisoned for his blasphemous writings. When Wilberforce took out a small Bible, Carlile said, "I wish to have nothing to do with that book; and you cannot wonder at this, for if that book be true, I am damned forever!" To which Wilberforce replied, "No, no, Mr. Carlile, according to that book, there is hope for all who will seek for mercy and forgiveness; for it assures us that God hath no pleasure in the death of him that dieth."[7]

Missions and Mercy Across the Miles

His zeal for the gospel and his compassion for perishing people were extended from personal relationships at home to places as far away as India. On April 14, 1806, he wrote, "Next to the Slave Trade, I have long thought our making no effort to introduce the blessings of religious and moral improvement among our subjects in the East, the greatest of our *national* crimes."[8] Seven years later "Wilberforce . . .

---

[5] Ibid., 119.
[6] Ibid., 205.
[7] Ibid., 258.
[8] Ibid., 235.

enthralled the House . . . with the cause of Christian missions in India."[9] The Englishman William Carey had to live in Serampore, a Danish enclave in India, until Wilberforce triumphed in 1813 when the prohibition of evangelism in British colonies in India was lifted by the East India Company Charter, which now guaranteed liberty to propagate the Christian Faith. "Parliament had opened a fast-locked door and it was Wilberforce who had turned the key, in a speech which Lord Erskine said 'deserves a place in the library of every man of letters, even if he were an atheist.'"[10] Even at this huge distance Wilberforce brought together evangelistic zeal and concern for social justice. He bemoaned the practice of *suttee* and would read out at his supper table the names of women who had been killed on the funeral fires of their husband; he knew something of the tyrannies of the caste system.[11]

The link that Wilberforce saw between social good and eternal good is seen in the case of the remote English people of Mendip Hills. In 1789, when Wilberforce saw the terrible plight of these backward, poor, unpastored people, he urged the philanthropist Hannah More to conceive a plan that he would pay for. She worked out a plan to establish a school and teach them to read. She wrote to Wilberforce, "What a comfort I feel in looking around on these starving and half-naked multitudes, to think that by your liberality many of them may

---

[9] Ibid., 235-36.
[10] Ibid., 238.
[11] Ibid., 236.

be fed and clothed; and O if but one soul is rescued from eternal misery how we may rejoice over it in another state!"[12]

The breadth of his heart and the diversity of his action beckon us all the more to ponder the source of his constancy, especially in a cause that was at first unpopular and easily defeated—the economically advantageous slave trade.

---

[12] Ibid., 92-93.

Chapter Four

Extraordinary Endurance

*C*onsider now the remarkable perseverance of this man in the cause of justice. I admit, this is what drew me to Wilberforce in the first place—his reputation as a man who simply would not give up when the cause was just.

There was a ray of hope in 1804 that things might be moving to a success (three years before it actually came), but Wilberforce wrote, "I have been so often disappointed, that I rejoice with trembling and shall scarcely dare to be confident till I actually see the Order in the Gazette."[1] But these repeated defeats of his plans did not defeat *him*. His adversaries complained that "Wilberforce jumped up whenever they knocked him down."[2] One of them in particular put it like this: "It is necessary to watch him as he is blessed with a very sufficient quantity of that Enthusiastic spirit, which is so far from yielding that it grows more vigorous from blows."[3]

---

[1] Ibid., 189.
[2] Ibid., 123.
[3] Ibid., 105.

When John Wesley was eighty-seven years old (in 1791) he wrote to Wilberforce and said, "Unless God has raised you up for this very thing, you will be worn out by the opposition of man and devils. But if God be for you, who can be against you."[4] Two years later Wilberforce wrote in a letter, "I daily become more sensible that my work must be affected by constant and regular exertions rather than by sudden and violent ones."[5] In other words, with fifteen years to go in the first phase of the battle, he knew that only a marathon mentality, rather than a sprint mentality, would prevail in this cause.

Six years later in 1800, on his forty-first birthday, as he rededicated himself to his calling, he prayed, "Oh Lord, purify my soul from all its stains. Warm my heart with the love of thee, animate my sluggish nature and fix my inconstancy, and volatility, that I may not be weary in well doing."[6] God answered that prayer, and the entire Western world may be glad that Wilberforce was granted constancy and perseverance in his labors, especially his endurance in the cause of justice against the sin of slavery and racism.

Obstacles

What makes Wilberforce's perseverance through four decades of political action in the single-minded cause of justice so remarkable is not only the length of it but the obstacles he had to surmount in the battle for abolition of the slave trade and

---

[4] Ibid.
[5] Ibid., 116
[6] Ibid., 179.

then of slavery itself. I have mentioned the massive financial interests on the other side, both personal and national. It seemed utterly unthinkable to Parliament that Britain could prosper without what the plantations of the West Indies provided. Then there were the international politics and how Britain was positioned in relation to France, Portugal, Brazil, and the new nation, the United States of America. If one nation, like Britain, unilaterally abolished the slave trade, but the others did not, it would simply mean—so the argument ran—that power and wealth would be transmitted to the other nations and Britain would be weakened internationally.

Slander

In February 1807, when Wilberforce, at forty-seven, led the first victory over the slave trade, it was true that as John Pollock says, "His achievement brought him a personal moral authority with public and Parliament above any living man."[7] But, as every public person knows, and as Jesus promised,[8] the best of men will be maligned for the best of actions.

On one occasion in 1820, thirteen years after the first victory, he took a very controversial position with regard to Queen Caroline's marital unfaithfulness and experienced a dramatic public outrage against him. He wrote in his diary on July 20, 1820, "What a lesson it is to a man not to set his heart

---

[7] Ibid., 215. Wilberforce's own assessment of the resulting moral authority was this (written in a letter March 3, 1807): "The authority which the great principles of justice and humanity have received will be productive of benefit in all shapes and directions."

[8] Matthew 10:25, "If they have called the master of the house Beelzebul, how much more will they malign those of his household."

on low popularity when after 40 years [of] disinterested pub-
lic service, I am believed by the Bulk to be a Hypocritical
Rascal. O what a comfort it is to have to fly for refuge to a
God of unchangeable truth and love."[9]

Probably the severest criticism he ever received came in
August 1823 from a slavery-defending adversary named
William Cobbett, who turned Wilberforce's commitment to
abolition into a moral liability by claiming that Wilberforce
pretended to care for slaves from Africa but cared nothing
about the "wage slaves"—the wretched poor of England.

> You seem to have a great affection for the fat and lazy and
> laughing and singing and dancing Negroes. . . . [But] Never
> have you done one single act in favor of the laborers of this
> country [a statement Cobett knew to be false]. . . . You
> make your appeal in Picadilly, London, amongst those who
> are wallowing in luxuries, proceeding from the labor of the
> people. You should have gone to the gravel-pits, and made
> your appeal to the wretched creatures with bits of sacks
> around their shoulders, and with hay-bands round their
> legs; you should have gone to the roadside, and made your
> appeal to the emaciated, half-dead things who are there
> cracking stones to make the roads as level as a die for the
> tax eaters to ride on. What an insult it is, and what an
> unfeeling, what a cold-blooded hypocrite must he be that
> can send it forth; what an insult to call upon people under
> the name of free British laborers; to appeal to them in behalf
> of Black slaves, when these free British laborers; these poor,
> mocked, degraded wretches, would be happy to lick the

dishes and bowls, out of which the Black slaves have break-fasted, dined, or supped.[10]

A Father's Pain

But far more painful than any of these criticisms were the heartaches of family life. Every leader knows that almost any external burden is bearable if the family is whole and happy. But when the family is torn, all burdens are doubled. Wilberforce and his wife Barbara were very different. "While he was always cheerful, Barbara was often depressed and pessimistic. She finally worried herself into very bad health which lasted the rest of her life." And other women who knew her said she "whined when William was not right beside her."[11]

When their oldest, William, was at Trinity College, Cambridge, he fell away from the Christian faith and gave no evidence of the precious experience his father called "the great change." Wilberforce wrote on January 10, 1819, "O that my poor dear William might be led by thy grace, O God." On March 11 he poured out his grief:

> Oh my poor Willm. How strange he can make so miserable those who love him best and whom really he loves. His soft nature makes him the sport of his companions, and the wicked and idle naturally attach themselves like dust and cleave like burrs. I go to pray for him. Alas, could I love my Savior more and serve him, God would hear my prayer and turn his heart.[12]

---

[10] Ibid., 287.
[11] Everett, *Freedom Fighter*, 64-65.
[12] Pollock, *Wilberforce*, 267.

He got word from Henry Venn that William was not reading for his classes at Cambridge but was spending his father's
allowance foolishly. Wilberforce agonized and decided to cut
off his allowance, have him suspended from school, put him
with another family, and not allow him to come home. "Alas
my poor Willm! How sad to be compelled to banish my eldest
son."[13] Even when William finally came back to faith, it
grieved Wilberforce that three of his sons became very high-
church Anglicans with little respect for the dissenting church
that Wilberforce, even as an Anglican, loved so much for its
evangelical truth and life.[14]

On top of this family burden came the death of his daughter Barbara. In the autumn of 1821, at twenty-two, she was
diagnosed with consumption (tuberculosis). She died five days
after Christmas. Wilberforce wrote to a friend, "Oh my dear
Friend, it is in such seasons as these that the value of the
promises of the Word of God are ascertained both by the
dying and the attendant relatives. . . . The assured persuasion
of Barbara's happiness has taken away the sting of death."[15]
He sounds strong, but the blow shook his remaining strength,
and in March 1822, he wrote to his son, "I am confined by a
new malady, the Gout."[16]

---

[13] Ibid., 268. From the diary, April 11, 1819.
[14] The official biography written by his sons is defective in that it portrays Wilberforce in a
false light as opposed to dissenters, when in fact some of his best friends and spiritual coun-
selors were among their number. After Wilberforce's death, three of his sons became Roman
Catholic.
[15] Ibid., 280.
[16] Ibid.

His Bad Eyes, Ulcerated Bowels, Opium, and Curved Spine

The word "new" in that letter signals that Wilberforce labored under some other extraordinary physical handicaps that made his long perseverance in political life all the more remarkable. He wrote in 1788 that his eyes were so bad "[I can scarcely] see how to direct my pen." The humorous side to this was that "he was often shabbily dressed, according to one friend, and his clothes sometimes were put on crookedly because he never looked into a mirror. Since his eyes were too bad to let him see his image clearly, he didn't bother to look at all!"[17] But in fact, there was little humor in his eye disease. In later years he frequently mentioned the "peculiar complaint of my eyes," that he could not see well enough to read or write during the first hours of the day. "This was a symptom of a slow buildup of morphine poisoning."[18]

This ominous assessment was owing to the fact that from 1788 doctors prescribed daily opium pills to Wilberforce to control the debility of his ulcerative colitis. The medicine was viewed in his day as a "pure drug," and it never occurred to any of his enemies to reproach him for his dependence on opium to control his illness.[19] "Yet effects there must have been," Pollock observes. "Wilberforce certainly grew more

---

[17] Everett, *Freedom Fighter*, 69.

[18] Pollock, *Wilberforce*, 81.

[19] Ibid., 79-81 for a full discussion of the place of opium in his life and culture. "Wilberforce resisted the craving and only raised his dosage suddenly when there were severe bowel complaints." In April 1818, thirty years after the first prescription, "Wilberforce noted in his diary that his dose 'is still as it has long been,' a pill three times a day (after breakfast, after tea, and bedtime) each of four grains. Twelve grains daily is a good but not outstanding dose and very far from addiction after such a length of time."

untidy, indolent (as he often bemoaned) and absent-minded as his years went on though not yet in old age; it is proof of the strength of his will that he achieved so much under a burden which neither he nor his doctors understood."[20]

In 1812 Wilberforce decided to resign his seat in Yorkshire—not to leave politics, but to take a less demanding seat from a smaller county. He gave his reason as the desire to spend more time with his family. The timing was good, because in the next two years, on top of his colon problem and eye problem and emerging lung problem, he developed a curvature of the spine. "One shoulder began to slope; and his head fell forward, a little more each year until it rested on his chest unless lifted by conscious movement: he could have looked grotesque were it not for the charm of his face and the smile which hovered about his mouth."[21] For the rest of his life he wore a brace beneath his clothes that most people knew nothing about.[22]

He Did Not Fight Alone

What were the roots of Wilberforce's perseverance under these kinds of burdens and obstacles? Before we focus on the decisive root, we must pay due respect to the power of cama-

---

[20] Ibid., 81.

[21] Ibid., 234.

[22] "He was obliged to wear 'a steel girdle cased in leather and an additional part to support the arms. . . . It must be handled carefully, the steel being so elastic as to be easily broken.' He took a spare one ('wrapped up for decency's sake in a towel') wherever he stayed; the fact that he lived in a steel frame for his last fifteen or eighteen years might have remained unknown had he not left behind at the Lord Calthorpe's Suffolk home, Ampton Hall, the more comfortable of the two. 'How gracious is God,' Wilberforce remarked in the letter asking for its return, 'in giving us such mitigations and helps for our infirmities.'" Ibid., 233-34.

raderie in the cause of righteousness. Many people associate
Wilberforce's name with the term *Clapham Sect*. That term
was not used during his lifetime. But the band that it referred
to were "tagged 'the Saints' by their contemporaries in
Parliament—uttered by some with contempt, while by others
with deep admiration."[23] The group centered around the
church of John Venn, rector of Clapham, a suburb of London.
It included Wilberforce, Henry Thornton, James Stephen,
Zachary Macaulay, Granville Sharp, John Shore (Lord
Teignmouth), and Charles Grant.

Henry Thornton, banker and economist, was Wilberforce's
"dearest friend"[24] and cousin. In the spring of 1792 he "suggested to Wilberforce that they set up a 'chummery' at
Battersea Rise, the small estate that Thornton had bought in
Clapham. Each would pay his share of the housekeeping, and
this became Wilberforce's home for the next five years."[25]

At certain points these friends . . . resided in adjoining
homes in a suburb of London called Clapham Common,
functioning as one. In fact, their *esprit de corps* was so evident
and contagious that whether geographically together or not,
they operated like "a meeting which never adjourned." The
achievement of Wilberforce's vision is largely attributable to
the value he and his colleagues placed on harnessing their
diverse skills while submitting their egos for the greater public good.[26]

---

[23] J. Douglas Holladay, "A Life of Significance," in *Character Counts*, 72.
[24] Pollock, *Wilberforce*, 102.
[25] Ibid., 117.
[26] Holladay, "A Life of Significance," 72.

Wilberforce did not set out to gather a strategic band of comrades to strengthen his cause. It came together because of the kind of man he was and the compelling vision he had of what a public Christian life should be. He had a deep "love of conversation and could hardly resist prolonging a chat and kept many late hours leaving the mornings to less important things."[27] This love of company and great capacity for friendship combined with the power of his vision for public righteousness to attract "the Saints." Together they accomplished more than any could have done on his own. "William Wilberforce is proof that a man can change his times, though he cannot do it alone."[28]

---

[27] Pollock, *Wilberforce*, 118-19.
[28] Pollock, "A Man Who Changed His Times," 88.

Chapter Five

The Deeper Root of Childlike Joy

*T*here is a deeper root of Wilberforce's endurance than camaraderie. It is the root of childlike, child-loving, self-forgetting joy in Christ. The testimonies and evidence of this in Wilberforce's life are many. A certain Miss Sullivan wrote to a friend about Wilberforce around 1815: "By the tones of his voice and expression of his countenance he showed that *joy* was the prevailing feature of his own mind, joy springing from entireness of trust in the Savior's merits and from love to God and man. . . . His joy was quite penetrating."[1]

On the occasion of Wilberforce's death, Joseph Brown spoke in St. Paul's Church in Middlesex. He focused on this attribute of the man:

---

[1] Ibid., 152.

He was also a most cheerful Christian. His harp appeared to be always in tune; no "gloomy atmosphere of a melancholy moroseness" surrounded him; his sun appeared to be always shining: hence he was remarkably fond of singing hymns, both in family prayer and when alone. He would say, "A Christian should have joy and peace in believing [Rom. 15:13]: It is his duty to abound in praise."[2]

The poet Robert Southey said, "I never saw any other man who seemed to enjoy such a perpetual serenity and sunshine of spirit. In conversing with him, you feel assured that there is no guile in him; that if ever there was a good man and happy man on earth, he was one."[3] In 1818 Dorothy Wordsworth, sister of the famous romantic poet, wrote, "Though shattered in constitution and feeble in body he is as lively and animated as in the days of his youth."[4] His sense of humor and delight in all that was good was vigorous and unmistakable. In 1824 John Russell gave a speech in the Commons with such wit that Wilberforce "collapsed in helpless laughter."[5]

This playful side made him a favorite of children, as they were favorites of his. His best friend's daughter, Marianne Thornton, said that often "Wilberforce would interrupt his serious talks with her father and romp with her in the lawn. 'His love for and enjoyment in all children was remarkable.'"[6] Once, when his own children were playing

---

[2] *The Christian Observer* (London), January 1834, 63.
[3] Jay, *The Autobiography of William Jay*, 317.
[4] Pollock, *Wilberforce*, 267.
[5] Ibid., 289
[6] Ibid., 183.

upstairs and he was frustrated at having misplaced a letter, he heard a great din of children shouting. His guest thought he would be perturbed. Instead he smiled and said, "What a blessing to have these dear children! Only think what a relief, amidst other hurries, to hear their voices and know they are well."[7]

He was an unusual father for his day. Most fathers who had the wealth and position he did rarely saw their children. Servants and a governess took care of the children, and they were to be out of sight most of the time. Instead, William insisted on eating as many meals as possible with the children, and he joined in their games. He played marbles and Blindman's Bluff and ran races with them. In the games, the children treated him like one of them.[8]

Southey once visited the house when all the children were there and wrote that he marveled at "the pell-mell, topsy-turvy and chaotic confusion" of the Wilberforce apartments in which the wife sat like Patience on a monument while her husband "frisks about as if every vein in his body were filled with quicksilver."[9] Another visitor in 1816, Joseph John Gurney, a Quaker, stayed a week with Wilberforce and recalled later, "As he walked about the house he was generally humming the tune of a hymn or Psalm as if he could not contain his pleasurable feelings of thankfulness and devotion."[10]

---

[7] Ibid., 232.
[8] Everett, *Freedom Fighter*, 70.
[9] Pollock, *Wilberforce*, 267.
[10] Ibid., 261.

Interested in All and Interesting to All

There was in this childlike love of children and joyful freedom from care a deeply healthy self-forgetfulness. Arthur Wellesley, First Duke of Wellington (1769–1852), wrote after a meeting with Wilberforce, "You have made me so entirely forget you are a great man by seeming to forget it yourself in all our intercourse."[11] The effect of this self-forgetting joy was another mark of mental and spiritual health, namely, a joyful ability to see all the good in the world instead of being consumed by one's own problems (even when those problems were huge).

Wilberforce's friend Sir James Mackintosh spoke of that remarkable trait of healthy, adult childlikeness, namely, the freedom from self-absorption that is interested in the simplest and most ordinary things:

> If I were called upon to describe Wilberforce in one word, I should say that he was the most "amusable" man I ever met in my life. Instead of having to think of what subjects will interest him it is perfectly impossible to hit one that does not. I never saw anyone who touched life at so many points and this is the more remarkable in a man who is supposed to live absorbed in the contemplation of a future state. When he was in the House of Commons he seemed to have the freshest mind of any man there. There was all the charm of youth about him.[12]

---

[11] Ibid., 236.
[12] Holladay, "A Life of Significance," 74.

His Presence Fatal to Dullness

This must have been the way many viewed him, for another of his contemporaries, James Stephen, recalled after Wilberforce's death, "Being himself amused and interested by everything, whatever he said became amusing or interesting. . . . His presence was as fatal to dullness as to immorality. His mirth was as irresistible as the first laughter of childhood."[13]

Here is a great key to his perseverance and effectiveness. His presence was "fatal to dullness . . . [and] immorality." In other words, his indomitable joy moved others to be happy and good. He remarked in his book *A Practical View of Christianity*, "The path of virtue is that also of real interest and of solid enjoyment."[14] In other words, "It is more blessed to give than to receive" (Acts 20:35). He sustained himself and swayed others by his joy. If a man can rob you of your joy, he can rob you of your usefulness. Wilberforce's joy was indomitable and therefore he was a compelling Christian and politician all his life. This was the strong root of his endurance.

Hannah More, his wealthy friend and a co-worker in many of his schemes for doing good, said to him, "I declare I think you are serving God by being yourself agreeable . . . to worldly but well-disposed people, who would never be attracted to religion by grave and severe divines, even if such fell in their way."[15] In fact, I think one of the reasons

---

[13] Pollock, *Wilberforce*, 185.
[14] Wilberforce, *A Practical View of Christianity*, 12.
[15] Ibid., 119.

Wilberforce did not like to use the word "Calvinist,"[16] although the faith and doctrines he expresses seem to line up with the Calvinism of Whitefield and Newton,[17] was this very thing: Calvinists had the reputation of being joyless.

Lord Carrington apparently expressed to his cousin Wilberforce his mistrust of joy. Wilberforce responded:

> My grand objection to the religious system still held by many who declare themselves orthodox Churchmen . . . is, that it tends to render Christianity so much a system of prohibitions rather than of privilege and hopes, and thus the injunction to rejoice, so strongly enforced in the New Testament, is practically neglected, and Religion is made to wear a forbidding and gloomy air and not one of peace and hope and joy.[18]

---

[16] He disliked anything that "produced hard and sour divinity." He wrote in a letter on May 26, 1814, "There are no names or party distinctions in heaven." Though he wrote in 1821, "I myself am no Calvinist," he "urged the claims of Calvinist clergy for bishoprics." In 1799 he had written, "God knows, I say it solemnly, that it has been (particularly of late) and shall be more and more my endeavor to promote the cordial and vigorous and systematical exertions of all friends of the essentials of Christianity, softening prejudices, healing divisions and striving to substitute a rational and an honest zeal for fundamentals, in place of a hot party spirit." Pollock, *Wilberforce*, p. 153. More than once he was heard to say, "Though I am an Episcopalian by education and conviction, I yet feel such a oneness and sympathy with the cause of God at large, that nothing would be more delightful than my communing, once every year, with every church that holds the Head, even Christ." Jay, *The Autobiography of William Jay*, 298-99.

[17] Many of his closest and most admired friends were Calvinists—for example, Hannah More and William Jay. He used his influence to promote Calvinists to bishoprics. When he sought out a church to attend, he often chose to sit under the ministry of Calvinists—for example, Thomas Scott, "one of the most determined Calvinists in England" (Pollock, *Wilberforce*, 153), and William Jay. He believed in the absolute sovereignty of God over all the pleasures and pain of the world ("It has pleased God to visit my dearest wife with a very dangerous fever." Ibid., 179). He knew that his own repentance was a gift of God ("May I, Oh God, be enabled to repent and turn to thee with my whole heart. I am now flying from thee." Ibid., 150). He loved the essay on regeneration by the Calvinist John Witherspoon and wrote a preface for it (Jay, *The Autobiography of William Jay*, 298). As I completed his book, *A Practical View of Christianity*, I could not recall a single sentence that a Calvinist like John Newton or George Whitefield or Charles Spurgeon could not agree with.

[18] Pollock, *Wilberforce*, 46.

Joy Is Our "Bounden Duty"

Here is a clear statement of Wilberforce's conviction that joy is not optional: it is an "injunction . . . strongly enforced in the New Testament." Or as he says elsewhere, "We can scarcely indeed look into any part of the sacred volume without meeting abundant proofs, that it is the religion of the Affections which God particularly requires. . . . Joy . . . is enjoined on us as our bounden duty and commended to us as our acceptable worship. . . . A cold . . . unfeeling heart is represented as highly criminal."[19]

So for Wilberforce, joy was both a means of survival and perseverance on the one hand, and a deep act of submission, obedience, and worship on the other hand. Joy in Christ was commanded. And joy in Christ was the only way to flourish fruitfully through decades of temporary defeat. It was a deep root of endurance. "Never were there times," he wrote, "which inculcated more forcibly than those in which we live, the wisdom of seeking happiness beyond the reach of human vicissitudes."[20]

But What about the Hard Times?

The word "seeking" is important. It is not as though Wilberforce succeeded perfectly in "attaining" the fullest mea-

---

[19] Wilberforce, *A Practical View of Christianity*, 45-46. I cannot let these sentences pass without pointing out the poetic power of Wilberforce's diction. Did you notice how he put parallel consonant sounds together? "Joy . . . enjoined. Commended . . . as acceptable. Cold . . . criminal." This kind of thing runs through all his writing and signals a passion to make his words pleasing and effective even as they instruct.

[20] Ibid., 239.

sure of joy. There were great battles in the soul as well as in Parliament. For example, in March 1788, after a serious struggle with colitis he seemed to enter into a "dark night of the soul." "Corrupt imaginations are perpetually rising in my mind and innumerable fears close me in on every side."[21] We get a glimpse of how he fought for joy in these times from what he wrote in his notebook of prayers:

> Lord, thou knowest that no strength, wisdom or contrivance of human power can signify, or relieve me. It is in thy power alone to deliver me. I fly to thee for succor and support, O Lord let it come speedily; give me full proof of thy Almighty power; I am in great troubles, insurmountable by me; but to thee slight and inconsiderable; look upon me O Lord with compassion and mercy, and restore me to rest, quietness, and comfort, in the world, or in another by removing me hence into a state of peace and happiness. Amen.[22]

Less devastating than "the dark night" were the recurrent disappointments with his own failures. But even as we read his self-indictments, we hear the hope of victory that sustained him and restored him to joy again and again. For example, in January 13, 1798, he wrote in his diary:

> Three or four times have I most grievously broke my resolutions since I last took up my pen. Alas! alas! how miserable a wretch am I! How infatuated, how dead to every

---

[21] Pollock, *Wilberforce*, 82.
[22] Ibid., 81-82.

better feeling yet—yet—yet—may I, Oh God, be enabled to repent and turn to thee with my whole heart, I am now flying from thee. Thou hast been above all measure gracious and forgiving.[23]

Unwearied Endeavor to Relish God

When Wilberforce pressed his readers to "unwearied endeavor" for more "relish" of heavenly things—that is, when he urged them to fight for joy—he was doing what he had learned from long experience. He wrote:

> [The true Christian] walks in the ways of Religion, not by constraint, but willingly; they are to him not only safe, but comfortable, "ways of pleasantness as well as of peace" [Prov. 3:17]. . . . With earnest prayers, therefore, for the Divine Help, with jealous circumspection and resolute self-denial, he guards against, and abstains from, whatever might be likely again to darken his enlightened judgment, or to vitiate his reformed taste; thus making it his unwearied endeavor to grow in the knowledge and love of heavenly things, and to obtain a warmer admiration, and a more cordial relish of their excellence. . . .[24]

There was in Wilberforce, as in all the most passionate saints, a holy dread of losing his "reformed taste"[25] for spiri-

---

[23] Ibid., 150. He confesses again after a sarcastic rejoinder in the Commons, "In what a fermentation of spirits was I on the night of answering Courtenay. How jealous of character and greedy of applause. Alas, alas! Create in me a clean heart, O God, and renew a right spirit within me" (167).

[24] Ibid., 102-3.

[25] The word "reformed" does not refer here to "Calvinistic," but simply to a spiritual taste that was once worldly and now has been "re-formed" into a spiritual taste for spiritual things.

tual reality. This dread gave rise to "earnest prayers . . . resolute self-denial" and rigorous abstinence from anything that would rob him of the greater joys. He illustrated this dread with the earthly pleasure of "honor." "[The] Christian . . . dreads, lest his supreme affections being thereby gratified [with human praise], it should be hereafter said to him 'remember that thou in thy life-time receivedst thy good things'" (Luke 16:25).[26]

He speaks of "self-denial" exactly the way Jesus did, not as an end in itself, but as a means to the highest pleasures. The mass of nominal Christians of his day did not understand this. And it was the root of their worldliness. "Pleasure and Religion are contradictory terms with the bulk of nominal Christians."[27] But for Wilberforce it was the opposite. The heart and power of true religion—and the root of righteous political endurance—was spiritual pleasure. "O! little do they know of the true measure of enjoyment, who can compare these delightful complacencies with the frivolous pleasures of dissipation, or the coarse gratifications of sensuality. . . . The nominal Christian . . . knows not the sweetness of the delights with which true Christianity repays those trifling sacrifices."[28] That is what he calls true self-denial—"trifling sacrifices"— just as the apostle Paul called all his earthly treasures "rubbish, in order that I may gain Christ" (Phil. 3:8).

Joy in Christ was so crucial to living the Christian life and

---

[26] Ibid., 122.
[27] Ibid., 103.
[28] Ibid., 237.

persevering in political justice that Wilberforce fought for it with relentless vigilance. "[The Christian's] watch must thus during life know no termination, because the enemy will ever be at hand; so it must be the more close and vigilant, because he is nowhere free from danger, but is on every side open to attack."[29] Therefore, when we say that Wilberforce's happiness was unshakable and undefeatable because it was beyond the reach of human vicissitudes, we don't mean it was beyond struggle; we mean he had learned the secret of "the good fight" (1 Tim. 6:12), and that his embattled joy reasserted itself in and after every tumult in society and in the soul.

Rooting Joy in Truth in the "Retired Hours"

The durable delights in God and the desires for the fullness of Christ that sustained Wilberforce's life did not just happen. He speaks of "the cultivation of . . . desire."[30] There were roots in doctrine. And the link between life and doctrine was prayer. He spoke in his book on Christianity of descending to the world from the "retired hours":

> Thus, at chosen seasons, the Christian exercises himself, and when, from this elevated region he descends into the plain below, and mixes in the bustle of life, he still retains the impressions of his retired hours. By these he realizes to himself the unseen world: he accustoms himself to speak and act as in the presence of "an innumerable company of

---

[29] Ibid., 123.
[30] Wilberforce, *A Practical View of Christianity*, 122.

angels, and of the spirits of just men made perfect, and of God the Judge of all" [Heb. 12:22-23].[31]

He was writing here out of his own experience. He could not conceal from others his commitment to personal prayer and private devotion. This was one of the main focuses in the funeral sermon by Joseph Brown:

> Persons of the highest distinction were frequently at his breakfast-table, but he never made his appearance till he had concluded his own meditations, reading his Bible, and prayer; always securing, as it were, to God, or rather to his own soul, I believe, the first hour of the morning. Whoever surrounded his breakfast-table, however distinguished the individuals, they were invited to join the family circle in family prayer. In reference to his own soul, I am informed, he set apart days, or a part of them, on which he had received particular mercies, for especial prayer. Not only did he pray in his closet, and with his family but if his domestics were ill, at their bed-side—there was their valued master praying with them—praying for them.[32]

He counseled his readers to "rise on the wings of contemplation, until the praises and censures of men die away upon the ear, and the still small voice of conscience is no longer drowned by the din of this nether world."[33] So the question is: contemplation on what? Where did Wilberforce go to

---

[31] Ibid., 123.
[32] *The Christian Observer* (London), January 1834, 63.
[33] Wilberforce, *A Practical View of Christianity*, 122.

replenish his soul? If his childlike, child-loving, self-forgetting, indomitable joy was a life-giving root for his endurance in the lifelong fight for abolition, what, we might say, is the root of the root? Or what was the solid ground where the root was planted?

Chapter Six

||||||||||||||||||||||||||||||||||||||||||||||||||||||||||||||||||||||||||||||||||||||||||||||||||||||

The Gigantic Truths of the Gospel

||||||||||||||||||||||||||||||||||||||||||||||||||||||||||||||||||||||||||||||||||||||||||||||||||||||

The main burden of Wilberforce's book *A Practical View of Christianity* is to show that true Christianity, which consists in these new, indomitable spiritual affections for Christ, is rooted in the great doctrines of the Bible about sin and Christ and faith.[1] "Let him then who would abound and grow in this Christian principle, be much conversant with the great doctrines of the Gospel."[2] "From the neglect of these peculiar doctrines arise the main practical errors of the bulk of professed Christians. These gigantic truths retained in view, would put to shame the littleness of their dwarfish morality. . . . The whole superstructure of Christian morals is grounded on their deep and ample basis."[3] There is a "perfect harmony between the leading doctrines and the practical pre-

---

[1] Wilberforce, *A Practical View of Christianity*, 118.
[2] Ibid., 170.
[3] Ibid., 166-67.

cepts of Christianity."[4] And thus it is a "fatal habit"—so common in his day and ours—"to consider Christian morals as distinct from Christian doctrines."[5]

Christ Our Righteousness

More specifically, it is the achievement of God through the death of Christ that is at the center of "these gigantic truths" leading to the personal and political reformation of morals. The indomitable joy that carries the day in time of temptation and trial is rooted in the cross of Christ. If we would fight for joy and endure to the end in our struggle with sin, we must know and embrace the full meaning of the cross.

> If we would . . . rejoice in [Christ] as triumphantly as the first Christians did; we must learn, like them to repose our entire trust in him and to adopt the language of the apostle, "God forbid that I should glory, save in the cross of Jesus Christ" [Gal. 6:14], "who of God is made unto us wisdom and righteousness, and sanctification, and redemption" [1 Cor. 1:30].[6]

In other words, the joy that triumphs over all obstacles and perseveres to the end in the battle for justice is rooted most centrally in the doctrine of justification by faith. Wilberforce says that all the spiritual and practical errors of the nominal

---

[4] Ibid., 182.
[5] Ibid., 198.
[6] Ibid., 66.

Christians of his age—the lack of true religious affections and moral reformation—

RESULT FROM THE MISTAKEN CONCEPTION ENTERTAINED OF THE FUNDAMENTAL PRINCIPLES OF CHRISTIANITY. They consider not that Christianity is a scheme "for justifying the ungodly" [Rom. 4:5], by Christ's dying for them "when yet sinners" [Rom. 5:6-8], a scheme "for reconciling us to God—when enemies [Rom. 5:10]; and for making the fruits of holiness the effects, not the cause, of our being justified and reconciled.[7]

Politician with a Passion for Pure Doctrine

It is a stunning thing that a politician and a man with no formal theological education should not only *know* the workings of God in justification and sanctification, but *consider them so utterly essential* for Christian living and public virtue. Many public people *say* that changing society requires changing people, but few show the depth of understanding Wilberforce did concerning *how* that comes about. For him, the right grasp of the central doctrine of justification and its relation to sanctification—an emerging Christlikeness in private and public—were essential to his own endurance and for the reformation of the morals of England.

This was why he wrote *A Practical View of Christianity*. The "bulk" of Christians in his day were "nominal," he observed, and what was the root difference between the nom-

---

[7] Ibid., 64. Emphasis added, but the capitalization is his emphasis.

inal and the real? It was this: The nominal pursued morality (holiness, sanctification) without first relying utterly on the free gift of justification and reconciliation by faith alone based on Christ's blood and righteousness. "The grand distinction which subsists between the true Christian and all other Religionists (the class of persons in particular whom it is our object to address) is concerning the *nature* of holiness, and the *way in which it is to be obtained.*"[8] What they do not see is that there must be a reconciliation with God and an imputed righteousness from him *before* we can live holy and righteous lives in the world. This was all-important to Wilberforce.

He saw that the nominal Christians of his day had the idea that "[morality] is to be *obtained* by their own natural unassisted efforts: or if they admit some vague indistinct notion of the assistance of the Holy Spirit, it is unquestionably obvious on conversing with them that this does not constitute the *main practical* ground of their dependence."[9] They don't recognize what constitutes a true Christian—namely, his renouncing "with indignation every idea of attaining it by his own strength. All his hopes of possessing it rest altogether on the divine assurances of the operation of the Holy Spirit, in those who cordially embrace the Gospel of Christ."[10]

This gospel that must be "cordially" embraced (that is, with the heart and affections, not just the head) is the good news that reconciliation and a righteous standing with God

---

[8] Ibid., 166.
[9] Ibid.
[10] Ibid.

precede and ground even the Spirit-given enabling for practical holiness. "The true Christian . . . knows therefore that this holiness is not to *precede* his reconciliation to God, and be its CAUSE; but to FOLLOW it, and be its EFFECT. That, in short, it is by FAITH IN CHRIST only that he is to be justified in the sight of God."[11] In this way alone does a person become "entitled to all the privileges which belong to this high relation," which include in this earthly life a "partial renewal after the image of his Creator," and in the life to come "the more perfect possession of the Divine likeness."[12]

Perhaps Our Greatest Need

Is it not remarkable that one of the greatest politicians of Britain and one of the most persevering public warriors for social justice should elevate doctrine so highly? Perhaps this is why the impact of the church today is as weak as it is. Those who are most passionate about being practical for the public good are often the least doctrinally interested or informed. Wilberforce would say: You can't endure in bearing fruit if you sever the root.

From the beginning of his Christian life in 1785 until he died in 1833, Wilberforce lived off the "great doctrines of the gospel," especially the doctrine of justification by faith alone based on the blood and righteousness of Jesus Christ. This is where he fed his joy. Because of these truths, "when all around him is dark and stormy, he can lift up an eye to Heaven, radi-

---

[11] Ibid. Capitalization is his.
[12] Ibid.

ant with hope and glistening with gratitude."[13] The joy of the Lord became his strength (Neh. 8:10). And in this strength he pressed on in the cause of abolishing the slave trade until he had the victory.

Therefore, in all our zeal today for racial harmony, or the sanctity of human life, or the building of a moral culture, let us not forget these lessons: Never minimize the central place of God-centered, Christ-exalting doctrine; labor to be indomitably joyful in all that God is for us in Christ by trusting his great finished work; and never be idle in doing good—that men may see our good deeds and give glory to our Father who is in heaven (Matt. 5:16).

---

[13] Ibid., 173.